M000098743

GOOD NEWS

for LITTLE HEARTS

Ferne Godfrey

© 2020 FERNE GODFREY All rights reserved. No part of this publication may be reproduced, distributed, or transmitted in any form or by any means, including photocopying, recording, or other electronic or mechanical methods, without the prior written permission of the publisher, except in the case of brief quotations embodied

in critical reviews and certain other noncommercial uses permitted by copyright law. ISBN 978-1-09832-015-7

The best news in all of the world, boys and girls, is that God loves you, and He wants a personal relationship with you. He wrote a big book we call the Bible to tell us all about Himself and how we can know Him.

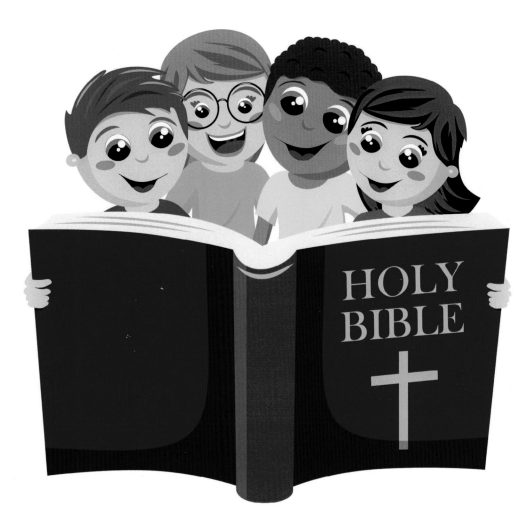

Let's look at some of His words from the bible and see how we can have this wonderful relationship with Him.

First, God who made the world, and God who made you, shows us and tells us how much He loves us.

Can you think of some ways He shows you His love? God is a loving God who cares for us and provides for us.

He is a good God but still we are separated from Him because of our sins. Do you know what sin is? Sin is anything we do that does not please God. Maybe we aren't kind to our brothers or sisters. Maybe we disobey our parents. Maybe we have told a lie.

Have you ever noticed that about yourself, that sometimes you do things that you should not do? We all sin, even grown up people sin. The bible says, "we all have sinned and come short of God's glory" (Romans 3:23).

Sin hurts people, sin hurts God, sin separates us from God. No one is perfect except God and His Son Jesus. If we want a relationship with God, something has to be done with our sin. The bible tells us that either our sin has to be punished or our sin can be forgiven.

Well here is some really good news! God made a way for our sins to be forgiven. But He made only one way. The way is through His Son Jesus. Jesus said, "I am the way, the truth and the life, no one comes to the Father except by me". (John 14:6)

This means if we want our sins forgiven and a right relationship with God, we go through Jesus. Jesus is the way. He is the doorway to God. The Bible says, God loved us so much that He gave His one and only Son, that whoever believes on Him will not perish but have eternal life. (John 3:16)

So God sent His Son Jesus, to the earth to be born as a special baby. Jesus lived a perfect life and took all of our sins upon Himself on the cross.

Jesus was punished so we would not have to be punished. Jesus died for our sins so we wouldn't have to die for our sins.

Jesus did all of the work, in fact, His last words on the cross were, "It is finished". He said those words to let us know that God's plan for our salvation was complete, nothing else needed to be done.

All we need to do is believe Him. "Believe on the Lord Jesus Christ and you will be saved," (Acts 16:31) Believe what God had Jesus do for us. Believe God's plan for our salvation.

Believe Jesus died for your sins so you don't have to be punished for them. God's word says, when we were sinners christ died for us (Romans 5:8).

Here's more good news, Jesus not only died for our sins and was buried, but three days later He came back to life.

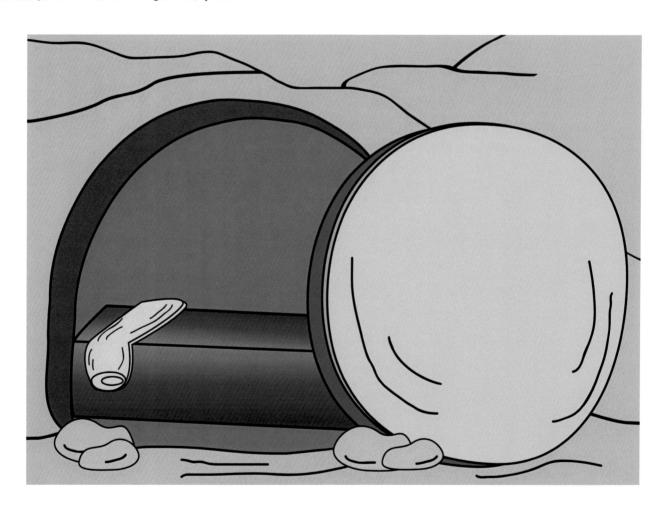

"He (Jesus) was buried and He was raised from the dead on the third day" (I Corinthians 15:4) Jesus can do anything! He has power over everything, even life and death! See what a great God we have!

After He got out of the grave, Jesus went about for 40 days visiting with his family and friends showing them that He was alive.

Then He told them to go tell others about the good news of salvation, about how to have their sins forgiven and how to have a right relationship with God.

Then it was time for Jesus to go back to heaven to be with God, His father. Now Jesus is in heaven.

Even though He is in heaven, He is watching over us. He is listening to our prayers. He is guiding our lives.

Boys and girls, this is good news! This is the gospel story. God sent Jesus on a rescue mission to come to earth, to die for our sins.

All we need to do is believe what Jesus did! Tell Him you want your sins forgiven and you want a right relationship with God.

Believe all that He said and thank Him for what He has done. There is much more we can learn about our wonderful God and how much He loves us. But the important first step is to believe. Believe Jesus to forgive your sins.

Be thankful Jesus did all the work, and remember His last words on the cross, "It is finished". See how much God loves us. He made all of the arrangements for us to be forgiven and to be part of His family. The bible says, God cannot lie.

Thank you, Jesus, for all you did for me on the cross!

STUDY QUESTIONS

Who does God love?

Who is perfect?

Are you perfect?

What is sin?

Sin must be punished or sin can be _____ (forgiven)

Who was punished for our sin?

What was the last thing Jesus said on the cross?

Why do you think he said that?

How many ways did God make for our sins to be forgiven?

Who is the doorway to God?

FERNE GODFREY is a graduate of East Tennessee State University, and a retired dental hygienist. She is a pastors wife, mother of two grown daughters and grandmother of two little boys (Lincoln and Winston) to whom she dedicates this book.